Th

THE IRISH
HARP EMBLEM

SÉAMAS Ó BRÓGÁIN

WOLFHOUND PRESS
& in the US and Canada
The Irish American Book Company

First published in 1998 by
Wolfhound Press Ltd
68 Mountjoy Square
Dublin 1, Ireland
Tel: (353-1) 874 0354
Fax: (353-1) 872 0207

Published in the US and Canada by
The Irish American Book Company
6309 Monarch Park Place
Niwot, Colorado 80503
USA
Tel: (303) 652-2710
Fax: (303) 652-2689

Wolfhound Press receives financial assistance from the Arts Council/An Comhairle
Ealaíon, Dublin.

British Library Cataloguing in Publication Data
A catalogue record for this book is available from the British Library.

ISBN 0-86327-635-0

Editorial Consultant: Roberta Reeners
Design and Origination: Design Image
Cover Illustration: Nicola Emoe
Cover Design: Slick Fish Design, Dublin
Printed in the Republic of Ireland by Colour Books, Dublin

CONTENTS

ONE

THE IRISH HARP

The Irish harp is the only national emblem in the world that consists of a musical instrument. In 1922, when the antiquarian George Sigerson was consulted on a design for the state seal of the Irish Free State by the Attorney General, Hugh Kennedy, Sigerson said of the harp:

It is now within the power of an Irish independent government to replace this emblem of humanising harmony in its high place of honour, unique and not undistinguished amongst the lions, the leopards, and the single and double-headed eagles of the rest of the world.[1]

With its distinctive shape, the Irish harp has been the most characteristic musical instrument of this country from at least the twelfth century.[2] The early history of the harp itself is obscure, although it undoubtedly evolved from the prehistoric lyre, which may have originated in ancient Egypt or Sumeria. The triangular or frame harp is a European invention; it may even have originated among the Celtic people. At an early stage in its history, it developed a distinctive form as well as a distinctive social role in Ireland that lasted up to the death of the traditional instrument at the beginning of the nineteenth century.

All the information available from early historical descriptions, as well as from mythology and folklore, makes it clear that the harp was a prominent feature of Irish life.

Mythology is replete with stories concerning harps and harpers. The Daghdha, a central divinity among the ancient Irish who appears as chief druid and later king of the mythical Tuatha Dé Danann, is credited with the ability to play the three kinds of magical music on the harp – *geantraí*, *goltraí* and *suantraí*. In this role, he appears in an early story involving an enchanted harp. At the second battle of Maigh Tuire (which supposedly took place in 1500 BC but in fact is a fable first recorded in the eighth century), the Tuatha Dé Danann defeated the invading Fomhóraigh. As the latter retreated, they took with them the harp belonging to the Daghdha's musician who, having succeeded in recapturing it, put the Fomhóraigh to sleep by playing magical music.

The harper Craiftine appears in a number of mythical stories. The famous folk tale concerning 'Labhraidh Lorc' (the mythical Leinster king Labhraidh Loingseach) and his ears is recorded from the tenth century down to the twentieth. The king had horse's ears, so every barber who cut his hair, thus discovering his secret, was put to death. Eventually Labhraidh could keep his secret no longer and told it to a certain willow tree. But Craiftine chose that very tree from which to have a new harp made, and when it was played it sang, 'Labhraidh Lorc has horse's ears!'[3]

Poets and musicians, including harpers, had very high status in early Irish society. According to the Féineachas or 'Brehon Laws' – the essentially authentic though embellished body of traditional law of the pre-Christian and Early Christian period – harpers had the highest standing among musicians within the *aos dána*, the artists' and craftsmen's class. This status was retained informally up to at least the seventeenth century: in their history of Ireland,

'Annála Ríochta Éireann' (1636), the Four Masters record the deaths of individual harpers by name.

'Both Barde, and Harper, is preparde, which by their cunning art,
Doe strike and cheare up all the gestes, with comfort at the hart.'
A sixteenth-century harper playing to a chief, from Derricke's Image
of Ireland.

The famous woodcut accompanying John Derricke's verse description *Image of Ireland* (1581), though absurdly inaccurate in its depiction of the harp, shows the role and status of the harper as he plays for the chief while the bard declaims his prowess.[4] In his *Chronicles* (1587), Holinshed describes a similar scene:

> *Their noble men, and noblemens tenants, now and then make a set feast, which they call coshering [cóisireacht], whereto flock all their reteiners, whom they name followers, their rithmours [rhymers], their bards, their harpers that feed them with musike: and when the harper twangeth or singeth a song, all the companie must be whist, or else he chafeth like a cutpursse, by reason his harmonie is not had in better praise.*[5]

There is conflicting evidence on the social role of harpers and their music in the seventeenth century, perhaps reflecting the turbulent political events of those years. With the collapse of the native order after the Battle of Kinsale in 1601, traditional musicians seem to have been regarded at first as outlaws. According to one source,

> *in 1603 a proclamation was issued by the Lord President of Munster [Henry Brouncker] for the extermination by martial law of: 'all manner of bards, harpers, etc.', and within ten days of it Queen Elizabeth herself ordered Lord Barrymore: 'to hang the harpers wherever found.' All through the seventeenth century they were proscribed and banned, hunted and persecuted.[6]*

The same source states that, under Cromwell – admittedly a special case – all harpers and other musicians had to obtain permission from a magistrate before being allowed to travel through the country:

> *all musical instruments savouring of 'popery' were ruthlessly destroyed so that Archdeacon Lynch, a contemporary writer, was of the opinion that within a short time scarce a single harp would be left in Ireland.*

On the other hand, there is evidence that the new order made its peace quickly enough with the musical aspects of the traditional culture, though perhaps in a sanitised form. The new gentry – whether of native, 'Old English' or planter origins – were soon apparently cultivating the harp and its music. We are told, for instance, that

> *the Irish are much addicted to musick generally, and you shall find but very few of their gentry, either man or woman, but can play on*

the harp; alsoe you shall not find a house of any account, without one or two of those instruments, and they always keep a harper to play for them at their meales, and all other times, as often as they have a desire to recreate themselves, or others which comes to their houses, therewith.[7]

A similar account from a later period is given by an Englishman who visited the south of Ireland in 1673:

The Irish gentry are musically disposed, and therefore many of them play singular well upon the Irish harp …[8]

But with the destruction of the old society, the remaining traditional harpers became for the most part itinerant minstrels who travelled from one patron's house to another. The most famous of the seventeenth and eighteenth-century harpers, Toirealach Ó Cearúlláin (1670–1738), whose compositions are among the most popular and enduring in Irish music, is not a typical representative of this era. In fact, his blend of traditional and art music was the subject of some criticism from the last of the traditional harpers.

Eventually, despite belated efforts to revive it, the making and playing of the Irish harp, as it had been known for almost a millennium, died out at the beginning of the nineteenth century. Irish society had changed fundamentally, as had musical tastes, and it was no longer possible for a musician to earn a living by travelling from house to house in all weathers, depending on the patronage of a class that was itself in decline. The ultimate reliance on training blind boys to play the harp seemingly made a virtue of what had at first been an unfortunate necessity; it could not contribute to the continuance of a tradition that was already so attenuated. Despite the heroic efforts of Edward Bunting and others, notably by means of the Belfast Harp Festival in 1792 (attended, incidentally, by Theobald Wolfe Tone), our present knowledge of the stringing and tuning of the traditional harp, the methods of playing and even the airs that were played is based largely on reconstruction and conjecture. The harp of the modern revival – sometimes called the 'neo-Irish harp' – is not the same instrument, either in construction or method of playing, although it has been made to resemble it.

TWO

A SYMBOL OF IRELAND

There are many representations of harps in manuscripts and on Early Christian stone crosses from the eighth or ninth century onwards as the Irish harp took on its characteristic features. In nearly all of these, the harp is shown being played rather than appearing by itself, as in the well-known example of Breac Mhaodhóg, the eleventh or twelfth-century book-shrine dedicated to Maodhóg, the seventh-century Wexford saint.[1] In many of these representations, it is evident that the harper symbolises the prehistoric Hebrew king David, the Biblical harp-player and psalmist. However, it seems probable that the frequent occurrence of symbols of David and his harp and the prestige attaching to them reflect the high status of harpers and poets in contemporary Irish society rather than those of the Bible.

The first appearance of the harp as a graphic symbol representing Ireland is in a late thirteenth-century manuscript in French called (after one of

King David playing the harp on an eleventh-century bronze book-shrine, Breac Mhaodhóg, c. 1050–1100. [National Museum of Ireland.]

its present owners) the Wijnbergen Armorial.* This source became known to scholars only in 1930. The second part of the manuscript, which includes the coats of arms of the kings of various countries, was apparently compiled by a French herald in the court of King Philippe III le Hardi and dates from the period 1270–85. Among the very last of these is the coat of arms attributed to *le.Roi dirlande* [*the king of Ireland*], consisting of a yellow harp on a blue shield. The harp has the curved forepillar already characteristic of the Irish harp, and eight white strings. The dating of this manuscript puts the Irish harp among the ten oldest national symbols in the world.[2]

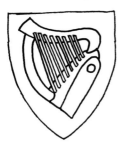

The coat of arms attributed to Ireland in the Wijnbergen Armorial, c. 1270–1285.

In addition to the well-known coats of arms of such countries as England, Spain and Portugal, the Wijnbergen Armorial contains the completely fanciful arms attributed to more distant countries and territories, such as Africa and Asia, that would have been known more by hearsay and legend than by accurate information. Into which category does Ireland fall? Perhaps some-

where in between. There could have been no authentic coat of arms of Ireland at that time, nor is it at all likely that this device originated within Ireland, as there was no *roi d'Irlande* or Irish state to display it. The only practical use which such a device could have had at that time would be by the English monarchy to

---

*An *armorial* or *roll of arms* is a manuscript illustrating the coats of arms of the feudal lords and knights of a particular region or those present at a particular battle.

represent its Irish dominions, for which use there is also no evidence.

Two possible factors combine to explain the original choice of this device as a symbol for Ireland. First, we know that it was already thought of in Britain and further afield as a distinctively Irish musical instrument, one that was characteristic of Ireland in a special way. The harp and its music were described in great detail and with uncharacteristic sympathy by Giraldus Cambrensis (Gerald de Barri), the Norman-Welsh priest – nephew of Maurice Fitzgerald, ancestor of the Fitzgeralds of Kildare; Cambrensis visited Ireland in 1184 and recounted his impressions and opinions in *Topographia Hibernica* (1188). John of Salisbury (*fl.* 1120–80), the English priest and philosopher who travelled extensively on the Continent and eventually became bishop of Chartres, refers to one of the crusades of the previous century and says there would have been no music if it had not been for the Irish harp.[3] The reference to Irish participation in the crusades comes as a surprise, but it does establish that the Irish harp was known at least at the time of writing. Secondly, it seems that a harp on a blue shield was the coat of arms attributed by mediaeval legend to the Biblical king David and so was available as a ready-made device for attributing to Ireland because of the significance of the harp.

But it was not for another two hundred years or more – as far as we know – that the harp coat of arms was used in any way by the English state to represent its Irish possession. In the meantime, a quite different device – a blue shield with three yellow crowns – was being used as the coat of arms of Ireland.

When Robert de Vere was created 'Duke of Ireland' by King Richard II of England in 1386, the three crowns device (within a white border) was to be added as an augmentation* to his own coat of arms, 'so long as he should be Lord of Ireland' (which was not very long, as it happened, as all his titles were forfeited two years later). As the coat of arms of Anglo-Norman Ireland, this device remained in use until at least 1487.

According to Bernard Burke, the nineteenth-century head of the Office of Arms in Ireland, the three crowns device was introduced by the Anglo-Normans following the invasion of 1172.

> *This coat [of arms] … was that of St. Edmund; and it is just possible that the Anglo-Normans, arrayed as they are known to have been under the banner of St. George and St. Edmund, may have introduced the bearings of St. Edmund as the ensigns of the newly-acquired country of Ireland. St. Edmund's arms had, indeed, been long employed as part of the royal insignia.*[4]

The three crowns device was used widely throughout mediaeval Europe, being attributed to several mythical saints and kings, as well as to some real ones who lived before the invention of heraldry. There are grounds for believing that the device originally represented the Three Magi, the Biblical 'wise men of the East'. This is the significance, for example, of its inclusion in the thirteenth-century coat of arms of the German city of Köln (whose cathedral possesses the supposed remains of the Magi). The same device was also attributed to the legendary and perhaps partly real Celtic chief Arthur, who may have opposed the Anglo-Saxons in Britain and who was to become the subject of so much

---

*An *augmentation* is an addition to a coat of arms by a monarch to symbolise an honour granted to the owner.

mediaeval legend and romantic literature. It was apparently for this reason that the device was later attributed also to St Edmund, one of the last kings of East Anglia, murdered by the Vikings in 870. On this basis, it was used as a supplementary device by King Edward I of England and his successors from at least the end of the thirteenth century. An identical device was

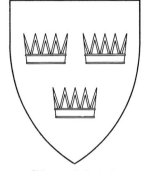

The arms of Norman Ireland: three crowns on a blue shield, now the coat of arms of Munster.

adopted in 1364 by King Albrekt of Sweden (Albrecht of Mecklenburg) as the coat of arms of the Swedish monarchy, which it remains.

Burke's hypothesis about St Edmund and the Normans seems credible, its stages being the attribution of the three crowns to St Edmund (a known fact), the Anglo-Normans' dedication to St Edmund (Burke's suggestion), and the rapid evolution of the arms of the Anglo-Normans' patron saint into the arms of their Irish province.

An Irish harp first appears in English usage about 1480, as a crest* attributed (posthumously) to King Richard III. In the College of Arms in London, there is a painting of a blue banner bearing a harp in a manuscript book from the period 1531–32.[5] But the decisive step in the widespread recognition of the harp

---

*A *crest* is an optional part of a coat of arms, placed above the shield (the definitive part of the coat of arms), usually on top of a helmet.

seems to have been its use by King Henry VIII on the Anglo-Irish silver groat (four pence) and half-groat from 1534[6] (a dating pioneered by Professor Michael Dolley)[7]; this was also the first time it appeared under a crown. A crowned harp featured on the Anglo-Irish coinage from this time until 1826, when a separate coinage for Ireland ceased to exist.

How or why did the three crowns give way to the harp? A popular tradition dating from the seventeenth century, apparently first recorded by the notoriously unreliable English commentator Fynes Moryson,[8] claims that King Henry VIII adopted the harp in place of the crowns to avoid any suggestion of the papal tiara or triple crown; but there is no evidence to support what historians have always regarded as a far-fetched idea. Perhaps, however, as the three crowns were at first arranged vertically more often than not, it is possible that they might have been so interpreted – or rather that the malicious could plausibly suggest that they might be.

An alternative explanation might be that there was some residual awareness of the harp attributed to Ireland in the Wijnbergen Armorial, with its implied precedence, or that this or a similar document was rediscovered about this time. Burke refers to a manuscript in the College of Arms in London, said to be in the handwriting of William Le Neve, 'Clarenceux King of Arms', and therefore dating from the period 1635–46, that states:

Note: y^e 3 crownes are y^e antient armes of Ireland (— the Harp but an antient badge or device of that country —) from whence it came y^t Vere, Duke of Ireland, had three crowns wth a border given him

in augmentation. In the tyme of Edw. ye 4th [1461–83] a commission being to enquire the arms of Ireland it was returned y^t y^e 3 crownes were the armes, and these arms I have seene upon the reverse of old Irish coynes.[9]

It is worth noting that up to this point, the harp as used by the English monarchy has not appeared on a shield but independently, whether with or without a crown. This suggests that, in heraldic terms, the harp was not a coat of arms but a 'badge', a device of rather more informal usage. King Henry VIII's decision to convert his

The crowned harp on the Anglo-Irish groat of 1534.

'lordship' of Ireland into a 'kingdom' from 1541 may have led to the adoption of a new coat of arms; this possibility could help to account for the overlapping usage of crowns and harp and would add credence to Le Neve's explanation.

Shortly afterwards, the harp appears on a blue shield on John Goghe's map of Ireland (1567) and on Queen Elizabeth I's charter to the city of Dublin (1583). A blue flag with a yellow harp appears on the map of Ireland in the chart produced by Augustine Ryther showing the routes of the defeated Spanish armada in 1588.[10] A seal of Queen Elizabeth I dated 1592 shows the harp again as a badge under the royal coat of arms. A blue banner with a yellow harp was carried at Queen Elizabeth's funeral in 1603.

King James I incorporated the harp on a blue field in the third
quarter of the royal arms and standard* of Britain in 1603; and
there it has remained to the present day. It is principally this usage
that has caused the harp on a blue field to be regarded throughout
this period as the coat of arms of Ireland, although, as we shall see,
it was not until 1945 that an Irish state adopted it.

*The coat of arms of the English monarchy,
incorporating the arms of Ireland.*

Why, incidentally, should the yellow harp so often have white
strings? There is a long tradition of adding a second colour to
certain heraldic devices, obviously to relieve the monotony of
uniformly coloured objects on a plain background: the heraldic

---

*A *standard* in modern usage is a flag flown to indicate the presence of a particular
person, especially a head of state.

lion, for example, almost invariably has a red tongue and claws, and similar standard variations exist for some other devices. On the other hand, the harp on the modern presidential standard has yellow strings (although this was not undisputed at the time of its adoption).

From about the time when the harp was incorporated in the British royal arms, graphic representations became more decorative, developing first a lion's head and then a forepillar in the shape of a woman – rather like a ship's figurehead – with the neck of the harp finally becoming a wing (a shape to which it lends itself well). This imaginative interpretation – sometimes called the 'Winged Maiden' or 'Maid of Erin' – flourished in the nineteenth century and remained popular, especially in American usage, up to the twentieth century.[11] These decorative varieties have no counterparts among real harps (although some Irish harps in the eighteenth century had a lion's head decoration). Nor is there any symbolic significance in the different types: it is merely a matter of artistic interpretation.

THREE

THE GREEN FLAG

O ne of the most significant developments in the history of Irish symbolism occurred in 1642, providing simultaneously the first use (as far as we know) of a harp on a green background and the first use of the harp emblem by representatives of the Irish nation itself.

In 1607, Eoghan Rua Ó Néill had left Ireland as a young man with his uncle, Aodh Ó Néill, in the 'Flight of the Earls' and had since been an officer in the Spanish army. In July 1642, he returned to lead the Ulster armies in the insurrection that had broken out in 1641. When Ó Néill's frigate, *St Francis*, returned to Dunkerque, its progress was reported by Matthew O'Hartegan, an Irish Jesuit based in Paris, to Luke Wadding, head of the Irish College in Rome. In his letter of 17 October 1642, O'Hartegan wrote:

> *Colonel Owne Ro his frigot is back to Dunkerk full of butter, tallow, and hides. This frigot bears the Irish harp in a green field in a flagg in the main-top.*[1]

Why did Ó Néill use a green field for his flag? It is tempting to suggest that the main object was to use any colour but blue – that the harp on a blue field would have been regarded then, as it has been ever since, as the symbol of the English domination of

Ireland. In the eighteenth century, the use of the harp on a blue background in the flags of some Irish regiments of the Spanish army is one counter-example, although green was also used here.[2] In fact, from the early Middle Ages up to the eighteenth century, there is a good deal of evidence that Ireland was identified with the colour green, at least in literary usage, because of its abundance of grass and foliage. One poem from the late seventeenth century refers to 'bratacha féaruaine na hÉireann' ('the grass-green flags of Ireland').[3] Somewhat later, Father Liam Inglis's comic poem 'Leastar an Bhráthar' (1757) refers to green as the colour of Ireland 'i dtaobh a harmais, machaire is cláirseach' ('because of its coat of arms, [green] field and harp').[4] This literary tradition of symbolism was to culminate in the popular name 'Emerald Isle', coined in 1795 by William Drennan in his poem 'Erin'.

Although Eoghan Rua displayed a green harp flag on his ship, the flags of the Catholic Confederates (1642–52) were generally white with a red cross; another type was green with a similar cross. Coins issued by the Confederates bore such a cross as well as other devices, but not a harp,[5] although a harp did appear – among other things – in the Confederates' seal. The harp on a blue field and also on a red field was a prominent motif on the flags of the Parliamentary (Cromwellian) forces.

Within thirty years of the display of Eoghan Rua's green flag, there is the first evidence of the legend of St Patrick and the shamrock. It appeared in the form of a coin or token, dated 1669 or 1670, and showed the saint holding up a trefoil[6] (although it is not until 1726 that we have the first explicit reference to this legend). Within a further ten years or so, there is the first known reference to the wearing of a green cross on St Patrick's Day, together with a leaf of shamrock (i.e. clover).[7]

The early history of the shamrock emblem is a mystery. As far as can be established, the tradition grew up that Patrick had used a leaf of shamrock to demonstrate the doctrine of the Trinity; this led to the wearing of a single shamrock leaf (not a 'sprig'!) on St Patrick's Day – at first in conjunction with the traditional cross. The wearing of a shamrock leaf might also have begun independently (perhaps because of its resemblance to a cross, as suggested by the archaeologist R. A. S. Macalister), leading in turn to the legend concerning Patrick. Both explanations seem unlikely, yet one of them must be true; on balance, the former seems more probable.

The first St Patrick's Day badges were red crosses (our earliest reference is from 1628);[8] by the end of the century, these crosses had generally become green. Did this change take place because of the conception of green as a national colour, or through the influence of the shamrock? Or was it that in the meantime, red had become associated with the 'redcoats' and so with English rule?

From about the same time, the harp on a green background was regarded as the coat of arms of the province of Leinster, a usage which has been ambiguous and confusing from the beginning. From the middle of the seventeenth century (the first documentary evidence is from 1644), coats of arms began to be attributed to the five provinces (the present four, together with Meath). Four of these – Ulster is the exception – share a rather strange feature: all were regarded at one time as the arms of

Ireland as a whole. (The arms later attributed to Connacht originated with the Schottenkloster or Irish monastery of Regensburg in Bavaria. They combined the eagle of the Holy Roman Empire with the crest from the arms of the Connacht sept of Uí Conchúir Donn or alternatively of Uí Briain of Thomond;[9] the colours and other details have since changed. A device of a king sitting on a throne, holding either a sceptre or a lily in his hand, was also described as the arms of Ireland in the middle of the sixteenth century; this in its turn was later assigned to the province of Meath.) What seems to have happened is this. At a time when it became customary for heraldic officials to attribute coats of arms to every territory and to every personality they could think of – including characters from ancient Greece and the Bible – the surplus stock of national symbols was plundered to provide ready-made though arbitrary devices for the provinces.

Despite the confusing allocation of the harp to the province of Leinster, the green flag with a yellow harp has been in effect the national flag of Ireland from at least the eighteenth century, yielding to the Tricolour only during the period 1916–19. An early corroboration of this usage is a coloured drawing of a flag for Ireland (in fact a civil ensign*) in the notebook of William Downman. Dated to 1685 or 1686, it consists of a green flag with a yellow harp and a canton† of St George's Cross.[10] This is the first of many manuscripts and flag charts, from the end of the

---

*A *civil ensign* is the flag of national identification flown by civilian ships, in some countries different from but in most countries identical to the national flag.

†A *canton* is a rectangular panel in the upper corner of a flag next to the flagstaff, often containing a miniature national flag. St George's Cross, the national flag of England – a red cross on a white field – was often added to other flag designs in this way.

seventeenth to the end of the eighteenth century, attributing this flag to Ireland. (Later flag charts also give the 'St Patrick's Cross' flag, a red diagonal cross on white. This is first recorded at the beginning of the seventeenth century as part of the design of the coat of arms of Trinity College, Dublin, and was introduced no doubt by analogy with St George's Cross for England and St Andrew's Cross for Scotland. Despite its subsequent appearance in flag charts over the years, there is no evidence that this flag was ever used in practice. Nor is there any connection, as far as we know, between this St Patrick's Cross and the red and later green crosses worn as badges on St Patrick's Day.)

A flag for Ireland, from the Downman *notebook, 1685 or 1686.*

The Volunteer movement of 1779–93, formed by sections of the Anglo-Irish ascendancy to fill the vacuum created by the departure of English regiments for America, provided the opportunity for the widespread display of the harp on flags and emblems – on blue, green and other backgrounds, sometimes crowned, sometimes not. Such flags were generally in the pattern of contemporary 'regimental colours', with elaborate designs containing many other devices, coats of arms, allegorical figures and mottoes.[11]

But the turning point in the development of the harp as a truly national symbol was undoubtedly its use by the Society of United Irishmen (1791–98) and particularly its display on green flags during the 1798 revolution. From 1795 onwards, the explicitly republican character of the United Irishmen is illustrated in its seal device, consisting of an elaborate harp with two slogans, *It is new strung and shall be heard* and *Equality*, the harp surmounted by a red cap of liberty.* To the great annoyance of the Volunteer leadership, the cap of liberty had already appeared over the harp in place of the crown in the emblems of some sections of the Volunteers.

Seal of the Society of United Irishmen, 1795–98.

Definite evidence that green was by now regarded as the national colour is provided by some incidents which preceded the uprising. On his return to Ireland from France in January 1793, Edward Fitzgerald – destined, though he had no inkling of it, to become one of the leaders of the United Irishmen and of the 1798

---

*A *cap of liberty* or *Phrygian cap* is a red conical cap based on that given to freed slaves in ancient Rome. It was used as a symbol of freedom in classical art and became particularly popular as a symbol of republicanism during the American and French Revolutions.

rising – took to wearing simplified dress as well as a green neckcloth (instead of the customary white), a habit which was significant enough to attract comment. On one occasion in the summer of 1794, while walking across the Curragh to his home in Kildare with his friend Arthur O'Connor, Fitzgerald was accosted by a number of British officers who took offence at his green neckcloth and demanded that he remove it. Fitzgerald and O'Connor – neither yet members of the United Irishmen – stood their ground; a fight was only narrowly averted.[12]

On 17 May 1798, a week before the final outbreak of the rising, one Anglo-Irish magistrate and yeomanry officer, Captain John Edwards of the Bray Yeomanry, wrote:

Where is the man whose blood will not boil with revenge who sees the petticoat of his wife or sister cut off her back by the sabre of the Dragoon – merely for the crime of being green, a colour certainly with them innocent of disaffection.[13]

A leaflet issued by the Leinster provincial committee of the United Irishmen on 19 April 1798 suggested that every company should have a green flag, measuring two feet square.[14] Of the flags actually used by the revolutionaries during 1798, there was no uniformity of design. Crosses and other devices were also used, together with backgrounds of other colours as well as a variety of mottoes and slogans – notably various versions of *Éirinn go brách**. But the underlying theme was the harp on a green field.[15] In Wexford, the leaders of the rising wore hat-bands with

---

*The popular use of the slogan *Éirinn go brách* [*Ireland for ever*] seems to date from this time, having previously appeared (as *Erin go bragh*) on the letter-headings of the Society of United Irishmen. ('Éirinn' is the ordinary name of Ireland in Irish; the modern official name 'Éire' is a dictionary word, an artificially preserved older form.)

the Irish harp drawn in gold leaf upon a green ground, encircled with the words Erin go braugh ...[16]

On 23 June 1796, Theobald Wolfe Tone, principal leader of the United Irishmen and one of the founding figures of Irish democracy, recorded in his diary a meeting with General Henri Clarke, a prominent French officer of Irish descent. They discussed the flag of the Irish unit of the expeditionary force being formed in France:

> *I said I should like very well to command two or three hundred of them, who might be formed into a corps of Hussars, to serve in the advanced guard of the army ... He seemed to relish this a good deal, and I went on to say that, in that case, they should be as an Irish corps in green jackets, with green feathers, and a green standard with the harp, surmounted by the cap of liberty. He bit at this, and made me draw a sketch of the device, and also a description, which he took down himself in French, from which I infer the standard will be made directly ...*[17]

Clarke clearly reported to the Directory immediately, because on the same day they wrote to General Lazare Hoche, commander of the ill-fated expedition to Ireland:

> *The Directory, not wanting to omit anything which may contribute to the success of the expedition to Ireland, to which they attribute the greatest importance, feel it their duty to advise you today, citizen general, of some details which must arrest your attention for a moment. The Irish, like every nation in the world, have a sort of religious respect for certain emblems, and principally those which led their ancestors into battle. It is possible to turn this respect and*

attachment for their ancient emblems to the advantage of the revolution which is being prepared in their country.

Consequently the Directory think that it would be expedient to have some colours and standards made, the field of which shall be green and in the centre of which a golden harp with silver strings* shall be displayed. This harp shall be surmounted by a cap of liberty and beneath it there shall be two sprigs of shamrock in saltire† as supporters ...[18]

This flag, or a similar one, was on board one of the ships of the fleet of the French Netherlands during its rash attempt to invade Scotland and Ireland when the vessel was captured by the English on 11 October 1797 at the Battle of 'Camperdown' (Camperduin).[19] Another Green Flag, no doubt similar, was taken after Tone's capture when the militia seized the contents of his ship, *Hoche*, at Buncrana on 31 October 1798. Sent to the Under-Secretary for Ireland, Edward Cooke, at Dublin Castle,[20] its later history is not known.

The draft of a proclamation in the handwriting of John Sheares, a United Irish leader who was captured on 21 May 1798 and hanged on 14 July in Dublin's Newgate Jail, declared:

Tone's design for a flag for the expeditionary force of 1797.

Irishmen – Your Country is free and you are about to be avenged. – That vile Government, which has so long

---

*Gold and *silver* are heraldic jargon for yellow and white, respectively.

†Crossed diagonally.

and so cruelly Oppressed you, is no more ... The National Flag the Sacred Green is at this moment flying over the ruins of Despotism ...[21]

Green flags, hat-bands and favours proliferated during 1798, and yet they were considered unusual enough for contemporary writers to feel the need to explain them, at least to English readers. The explanation put forward was that green had been adopted by the revolutionaries from the colour of the shamrock; but we already know of the prior existence of green flags from at least the middle of the seventeenth century. A more significant reinforcement of the use of green at this time was its explicit use to represent the 'Tree of Liberty' which symbolised both the American and French Revolutions. It included the wearing of green branches and the hanging of green boughs from windows and rooftops, widespread especially in Wexford throughout the rising.

One other ingredient that might be added to the mixture, though the most dubious, is the former traditional use of green as the colour of rebellion, or at least of radicalism. Used largely in England rather than Ireland, it is sketchily documented from at least the time of Cromwell (when green was the symbol of the 'levellers' or radical republicans) to the 1670s (when the Green Ribbon Club, a forerunner of the Whig party, organised anti-Catholic mobs in London). The underlying significance of this use is not known but may derive from the suggestion of fertility and therefore of renewal.

Robert Emmet, who in 1803 attempted to continue the revolution begun by the United Irishmen, had a flag similar to

George Cruikshank's drawing of the defeat of the insurgents at Vinegar Hill, Enniscorthy, in 1798. [Courtesy of the National Library of Ireland.]

that of the 1798 revolutionaries. Discovered after his arrest on 23 July 1803 and complete with the cap of liberty, it differed from Tone's flag in that instead of the shamrock, it had a ribbon bearing the slogan *Erin go bragh*.[22] Among Emmet's papers, a draft of a manifesto declared that 'necessary secrecy' had prevented him from giving notice of his plans but that

> *the erection of our national standard, the sacred though long-degraded green, will be found a sufficient call.*[23]

Throughout the nineteenth century and into the early years of the twentieth, what came to be known simply as the Green Flag – its yellow harp was understood – was the *de facto* national flag. Popular ballads in honour of the Green Flag, inspired by 1798 and 1803, flourished from the beginning of the nineteenth century to the middle of the twentieth, to be abandoned only in our own generation; they included 'The Wearing of the Green' and 'The Seanbhean Bhocht'.

> *And what colour will they wear? says the Seanbhean Bhocht;*
> *What colour will they wear? says the Seanbhean Bhocht.*
> *What colour should be seen where our fathers' homes have been*
> *But our own immortal green? says the Seanbhean Bhocht.*

Robert Emmet's flag, captured in 1803.

Practically all the revolutionary and other national movements of the nineteenth and early twentieth centuries – the Repeal Association, Young Ireland, the IRB and Fenians, the Home Rule movement, the Land League, the Irish Volunteers and the Irish Citizen Army – displayed the Green Flag (although in various forms and sometimes in combination with other devices), while its actual use was confirmed by innumerable references in literature and art. This use of the Green Flag reinforced, and was in turn reinforced by, the concept of green as the national colour, particularly as English rule in Ireland continued to be symbolised by the harp on a blue field. The use of the same symbol by both the colonial power and the nation itself made this distinction of background colour a vital one: in the words of G.A. Hayes-McCoy,

> *as far as symbolism is a guide to history, we may speak of the Irish*
> *struggle of modern times as one to remove the crown from above the*

harp and to place the harp itself on a green field instead of a blue one.[24]

There were only two significant exceptions to this demarcation. One was the harp on a blue ground on the flags of some of the Continental Irish regiments led by descendants of the Wild Geese. The other was the flag already referred to in which the harp on a green field was combined with a canton of St George's Cross (and later of the Union Jack). This flag (sometimes called the 'Irish ensign' and sometimes the 'Irish jack') was regularly included in flag charts and seems to have had a limited use as a kind of 'loyal' national flag.[25]

The flag of the Lord Lieutenant of Ireland, c. 1801– c. 1922

During this period, the official British use of the harp on a blue field took two principal forms. One is its continued inclusion in the arms and flag of the English monarchy, representing its claim to the territory of Ireland. The other was the flag of the

Lord Lieutenant of Ireland, the nominal head of the British administration in Ireland, which displayed a harp on a blue shield at the centre of the Union Jack. The first known reference to this flag is in a flag chart published in 1842; it presumably remained in use until the position ceased to exist on 16 January 1922.[26]

During the later part of the nineteenth century, the Green Flag itself seems to have been alternately suppressed and tolerated. Irish ships that flew the Green Flag, even briefly, instead of the British Red Ensign were forced to haul it down. In 1885, when Dublin City Council was prohibited from flying the Green Flag during the visit of Queen Victoria's son Edward, it promptly adopted a flag of its own which consists of the Green Flag with the addition of a canton of the city arms, which it flies to this day.

The flag of Dublin City Council, 1885 to date.

The Irish Volunteers formally declared the Green Flag to be the national flag. In 1914, the Provisional Committee for the Colours of the Irish Volunteers authorised designs for 'regimental colours' to be adopted by different units. In the report of this committee's recommendations, Michael O'Rahilly ('the O'Rahilly') wrote:

... The 'National' Colour shows on a green ground the Golden Harp of Ireland with its nine silver strings, which is, as a matter of fact, the National Flag of Ireland. Its antiquity is well established. It is

supposed to represent the mystic harp of Dagda, which, when he played, caused the four seasons to pass over the earth – a symbol of life that joyously renews itself.

Notwithstanding that the English government uses blue ground instead of green under the harp, the fact that Dagda's harp was called 'the oak of the two greens', and that Dagda himself was referred to as 'the green harper', as well as the universal consensus of Irish opinion, establish beyond doubt that the colours should be green.

On the advice of Dr. [George] Sigerson, the doyen of our antiquarians, the carved harp, or cláirseach, *bearing the figure of Erin, has been adopted in preference to the plain harp, or* cruit,* *which the Doctor believes should be only used for the Arms of Leinster.*[27]

The following year, on 10 March 1915, an order issued by Patrick Pearse, director of organisation, echoed uncannily the order to the United Irishmen 117 years earlier:

Every company of Irish Volunteers is to provide itself with an Irish Flag … The authorised flag is a plain gold harp on a green ground, and no other flag, except authorised regimental colours, is to be carried by bodies of Irish Volunteers.[28]

The Irish Citizen Army, revolutionary allies of the Irish Volunteers, also carried the Green Flag as the national flag, to

---

*This terminological distinction is not valid. From the beginning, the Irish name for the harp has been *cruit* (although this has been applied also to other stringed instruments) and later also *cláirseach* (a term that appears to have been used first in Scotland from the fifteenth century). Both words simply mean a harp, although there is a tendency for *cruit* to refer to the smaller (earlier) variety, while *cláirseach* is also applied to the orchestral harp. There is no special name for the ornamental harp with a figurehead.

accompany their own distinctive device, the Plough and the Stars. As a curtain-raiser to the rising that was to begin eight days later, the Citizen Army organised a 'Solemn Ceremony of Hoisting the Irish Flag' at Liberty Hall, Dublin, on 16 April 1916. In James Connolly's words,

A unit flag of the Irish Volunteers, 1914–1916.

on that day, the Irish Citizen Army, the armed forces of Labour … hoisted and unfurled the Green Flag of Ireland, emblazoned with the Harp without the Crown … the sacred emblem of Ireland's unconquered soul …[29]

A number of commentators have since suggested that this ceremony was a subterfuge: that Connolly was obscuring the arrangement he had entered into with the IRB to take part in an armed uprising.[30] No evidence is put forward for this assertion, which seems very improbable. But the use of the Tricolour (in addition to the Green Flag) during the rising itself does suggest that the IRB wished to promote it as the flag of the nascent republic, in place of the Green Flag of popular use. If this is so, their plan was successful, for by 1917, the Green Flag had been definitively replaced by the Tricolour, and it did not survive the creation of an Irish state.

The Tricolour (in various forms) had arisen spontaneously from 1830, under the influence of the July Revolution in France. It was formally proposed as a national flag by John Mitchel in an article in the *United Irishman* of 15 April 1848 and (with the colours orange, white and green) presented to a meeting in Dublin on the same date addressed by Mitchel and Thomas Francis Meagher. The Tricolour was employed to a limited extent from 1848 onwards, generally among the more militant elements of the independence movement; and there seems to be some basis for the belief that it was regarded as a more revolutionary or more republican emblem than the Green Flag.

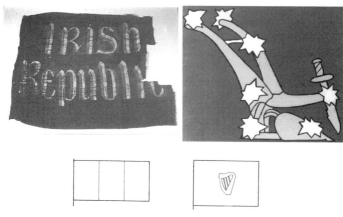

The flags flown by the 1916 insurgents in Dublin.

There is some uncertainty and some conflicting evidence about the flags displayed by the insurgents during 1916. The general picture is that both the Green Flag and the Tricolour were displayed, in approximately equal numbers, on the principal buildings occupied in Dublin.[31] The unique 'Irish Republic' flag flown on the GPO, with that name hand-painted on a green background, would certainly suggest that the leaders had no confidence in the capacity of either flag to convey a precise political message to the public – the principal function of a flag – and instead felt the need to resort to the rather crude practice of spelling out that message in words. But after 1916, a combination of circumstances seems to have led to the feeling that the Tricolour captured the mood of the times. Unlike the harp emblem, it had first arisen out of the national movement itself (although of foreign inspiration), while its tricolour design, with its explicit association with the French Revolution of 1789 and the other European revolutionary and republican movements, guaranteed that it would never be confused with any of the national emblems that were also used by the colonial power.

An additional factor in the rejection of the Green Flag may have been its use by John Redmond and his followers at the meetings organised to persuade Irishmen to join the British army to fight in the First World War. The simplicity of the Tricolour and the ease of manufacturing it may have added their small contribution in the first era in Irish history in which flags, most of them no doubt home-made, were displayed on a mass scale. As photographs and newsreels show, the sea of flags greeting the amnesty prisoners in June 1917 were all Tricolours. In 1922, the Irish Free State began the official use of the Tricolour. In 1926, the President of the Executive Council (head of government), William Cosgrave, replied to a Dáil question about its status that the Tricolour had become the national flag through usage. In 1937, the Constitution of Ireland formally declared it to be the national flag.

The Tricolour had first appeared largely as a response to outside events rather than to any significant development within the independence movement; it was almost by chance that it came to be taken up in the way it was. In 1916, it had the advantage of comparative novelty. Perversely, it may have been the very acceptability of the Green Flag to all sections of the Irish people – compared with the Tricolour's retrospective identification with the militants who led the rising – that contributed most to its rapid decline and rejection.

In our own time, as a result of partition and the polarisation this has created, the Tricolour has become *de facto* the flag of the 26 Counties and at the same time a partisan flag in the North. It is impossible to avoid the suggestion that the Green Flag will be the only serious candidate for the flag of a reunited Ireland.

FOUR

STATE SEALS

The first Irish state was the Irish Republic, established by Dáil Éireann on 21 January 1919 and brought to an end on 15 January 1922 as a prelude to the creation of the Irish Free State. In a Dáil debate on 24 November 1937, Éamon de Valera stated: 'On the old republican seal there was originally a harp.' This presumably refers to that period, although it is not clear what use the clandestine republic had for such a formality.

The short-lived Irish Republic gave way to the Provisional Government of 'Southern Ireland' (16 January to 5 December 1922) which preceded the formal setting up of the Irish Free State. It adopted for its seal a unique device, made up of disparate design elements. This displayed a quartered shield with the coats of arms of the four provinces, the shield placed on an uncial letter *E* (for Éire) and the whole within a frame consisting of the eight-pointed star and flames of the Irish Volunteers badge.

For a time, the quartered shield with the arms of the four provinces enjoyed a shadowy existence as a national device and still surfaces occasionally. From 1923, its use on one of the first series of postage stamps[1] contributed to a fairly widespread belief that it was the official coat of arms of Ireland: this is how it is described, for example, in the 1954 edition of the authoritative *Boutell's Heraldry* by C. W. Scott-Giles.[2] In the 1930s and '40s, this distinctive and rather attractive device was in fact a candidate in the private debate among civil servants about an official coat of arms, but it fell an early victim to the heraldic purists. (According to heraldic convention, a quartered shield can only be used to symbolise the union of dynasties through marriage. It is curious, therefore, that the most visible manifestation of heraldic

The Four Provinces postage stamp, 1923–1937, 1940–1968.

quartering in modern times – the British royal arms and standard – is essentially a symbol of union by conquest.)

The Irish Free State, which existed from 6 December 1922 to 28 December 1937, adopted the practice of using a harp on official seals, first on those of individual ministers, then of the Executive Council (government) as a whole. A letter of 13 January 1923 from the acting secretary of the Executive Council to all ministers records:

At the meeting of the Executive Council held on the 28th December last it was decided that the Celtic Harp should be adopted as the main theme of a design of Ministerial Seals …[3]

Later the same year, on 28 August 1923, the secretary of the Executive Council wrote to the secretary of the Ministry of Finance, Joseph Brennan:

I have to inform you that the 'Brian Boru Harp', a photograph of which was handed by the Attorney-General [Hugh Kennedy] to Mr. McElligott [assistant secretary of the Ministry of Finance] a few days ago, has been approved by the Executive Council as the basis of the Official Seal of the Government.

The seal of the Irish Free State, which was in use from 1924 until 1937, was designed by Archibald McGoogan of the National Museum. It consisted of an elaborate circular frame, approximately 6 inches (150 mm) in diameter, of a design taken from the base of the Ardagh Chalice. In the centre, between the words *Saorstát Éireann*, was a representation of the Trinity College harp, showing eighteen strings.[4]

This is the first time in our chronological survey that we have come across the explicit use of a particular harp as a model. Many earlier representations were drawn by people who had possibly never seen an Irish harp, and some bore scant resemblance to a real harp of any kind. The upsurge of interest in Irish history and archaeology during the nineteenth century led naturally to a desire for greater authenticity, and the result was a gradual adoption of models based on real Irish harps. The harp in the possession of Trinity College, Dublin, was identified as the oldest surviving instrument (although it is not as old as it was then believed to be), and harp emblems based on this design became increasingly common from the end of the nineteenth century.

The Trinity College harp has been dated to the fourteenth or fifteenth century; in the romantic past, it was given the completely fanciful title of the Brian Bórú harp, after the ard-rí who was killed at the Battle of Clontarf in 1014. Nothing is known for certain of its early history. It was presented to Trinity College in 1782 by William Conyngham of Slane Castle in a dismembered state, badly reconstructed some time after 1850, and professionally restored in 1961, at which time it was to some extent playable.[5]

The fourteenth or fifteenth-century Trinity College harp. [Green Studio]

The Trinity College harp is of the type musicologists call the small low-headed Irish harp, which was in use up to the early sixteenth century, and is one of three of this type to survive. It has an overall height of about 34 inches (0.86 m) and is made from willow, as were all the early Irish harps, its hollow soundbox carved from a single piece of wood. The traditional harp was played against the left shoulder and plucked with long fingernails. The Trinity College harp originally had thirty brass strings (brass in former times being rather closer to bronze); twenty-nine strings are now in place. The strings are fixed along the left-hand side of the neck and are not exactly parallel but slightly fanned out (a detail that is not reproduced in any graphic representations).

In the early years of the Irish Free State, William Butler Yeats, then a senator, sought the support of the Attorney General, Hugh Kennedy, for the establishment of

> *a committee of artists which would ensure that all the symbols of the new state – seals, medals, coins and so on – would carry the imprint of native Irish genius.*

Among the matters to which Yeats gave his attention were the wigs and gowns worn in the courts in imitation of those of England, believing they were 'part of the trappings of an alien regime which should be swept away.' Under Yeats's direction, a set of robes was designed by the English artist Charles Shannon; also submitted were designs by Kitty MacCormack of the Dun Emer Guild, all of which bore on the front a large harp on a green disc surrounded by a yellow ring. The whole project eventually fizzled out, although one set of robes was worn for a time in the District Court. Kennedy's reply in October 1926 to a letter from the historian Alice Stopford Green is interesting:

> *The de-anglicising of this country and the restoration of our own culture will try many souls to breaking point before (if ever) it is achieved. It is a task for the temper of a patient, persistent Cavour. The question of our robes is but an incident, a small passing test as we go on.*[6]

It was not yet the case, however, that the harp was accepted as the exclusive state badge, much less that the Trinity College harp was the only model. This is made clear by the procedures adopted in the introduction of the first modern Irish coinage, which went into circulation on 12 December 1928. In 1926, the Executive Council of the Irish Free State appointed a committee to advise on the design of the new coins, under the chairmanship of Yeats. At its first meeting, on 17 June 1926, the secretary of the Department of Finance, Joseph Brennan, announced that he wished

> to convey to the Committee three provisional decisions which had been arrived at by the Minister for Finance [Ernest Blythe] in regard to the coins, but which were not to be regarded as the final decisions of the Minister or the Government, or as binding on the Committee. These were:—
>
> (1) That a harp should be shown on one side of the majority of the coins, if not all …[7]

In their report of 6 August 1926, the committee stated:

It is our unanimous opinion that the obverse of every coin should consist of a harp, with the words 'Saorstát Éireann' and the date of issue; that the form of the harp should be based on the Trinity College, the Dalway or the Ullard harp; and that if feasible the same type of harp should appear on the obverse of all coins and the same design. The advantage of this uniformity is that the coins will be immediately and easily identifiable as Saorstát coins by their obverse … It is not recommended that artists should be compelled to adhere faithfully to the types of harp mentioned, in matters of detail, but rather that they be permitted to take any liberties they please, in order to produce a beautiful and dignified design …

The seven artists invited to submit designs were supplied with photographs of the harps known respectively as the 'Trinity College' and 'Dalway' harps (the Minister having decided against the less familiar 'Ullard' harp) …

In the event, the winning designs were those of the English sculptor Percy Metcalfe, whose interpretation of the Trinity College harp therefore became the feature of the obverse of all the coins and consequently – though this was not foreseen at the time – the model for all subsequent official interpretations of the harp emblem.

From 1938, following the adoption of the Constitution of Ireland the previous year, the inscription on the coins was changed from *Saorstát Éireann* to *Éire,* and the opportunity was taken to make some alterations in the details of the harp, including a reduction in the number of strings (presumably for technical reasons) from sixteen to fourteen.

It is a curious fact that the harp as invariably depicted in badges and on flags today is not exactly in profile, as is customary with graphic symbols of all kinds. Instead, it is shown in perspective, as seen from a viewpoint displaced slightly towards the front, which slightly foreshortens the harp and causes the front surface of the

The state emblem on the obverse of the modern coinage, 1928 to date.

triangular soundbox to be seen. This peculiar shape results from the fact that modern representations of the symbol are based on photographs supplied to the artists. Current official drawings have some other peculiarities: the forepillar and neck are reinterpreted as if they were in profile while the soundbox remains in perspective. And, because the photographs supplied seem to date from before the harp's professional restoration in 1961, they show a slightly distorted shape to begin with and a gratuitous ornamental extension to the bottom of the soundbox. (For comparison, a reasonably accurate profile drawing is included in the decorative design on the title page.)

The trivial detail of the number of strings to be shown in representations of the harp has caused problems from time to time. There is no single authentic number: the traditional harp seems to have had approximately thirty strings, and later types often had many more. Balancing the desire for authenticity are the severe limitations imposed by the scale of the representation and by the material used. Although artistic licence has traditionally allowed a representation of the harp to have any number of strings (sometimes as few as five or six), a dogmatic approach to this detail, as to others, was to lead to the altering of official drawings to represent the full complement of thirty strings originally belonging to the Trinity College harp.

The coming into effect of the Constitution also meant a change in the state seal. The Presidential Seal Act (1937) specifies the procedures for the custody and use of the seal, but not its design. A brief debate took place in Dáil Éireann on 24 November 1937, during which the question of a competition for a design was raised; but in the end it was decided – essentially on grounds of cost – to retain the Free State seal, changing only the inscription, from *Saorstát Éireann* to *Éire*. The number of strings on the harp was also changed, mysteriously, from eighteen to fifteen.[8]

The presidential seal, 1937 to date.

FIVE

THE PRESIDENTIAL STANDARD

The office of President of Ireland was created by Article 12 of the Constitution, which was adopted by plebiscite on 1 July 1937 and entered into force on 29 December the same year. The first president, Dr Douglas Hyde, was inaugurated on 25 June 1938.

The modern institution of head of state, as distinct from head of government, derives to a considerable extent from the concept of monarchy. Some of the popular notions about monarchs – such as the idea that they are 'above politics' – are commonly transferred to the holders of such offices; and the creation of a special flag for such officials seems to be part of this process. Given that the declared purpose of the presidential standard is to indicate the presence of this official in person, and the fact that no other personal flags, or indeed departmental flags, are provided for, it would seem that the use of such a flag is intended to invest the office, whose actual functions are minimal, with some of the mystique that is popularly supposed to attach to monarchy.

The idea of a flag for the presidency was first put forward on 28 June 1944 in a letter from the president's secretary, Michael McDunphy, to the Government secretary, Maurice Moynihan. McDunphy wrote:

It has been suggested to me on a number of occasions that there should be a Presidential Standard, and I must say that the idea appeals to me.

I would not favour the creation of an emblem totally distinct from the National Flag but think that the latter should be used as the basis.

There are many who regret the complete abandonment of the former national flag, the harp on a green, or more correctly, blue ground, and would like to see it restored in some form, and this very understandable feeling regarding the older flag could be met, without in any way conflicting with correct flag design, by superimposing on the white band of the national tricolour a small gold harp on a blue ground, the shape of the latter being a circle, an oval or other chosen form …

There is of course no urgency but I think that the idea is worth considering. If it were to be adopted, the entry of the second President on office might be an appropriate occasion for its inauguration.[1]

Moynihan replied:

I have discussed with the Taoiseach [Éamon de Valera] your letter … He agrees that the idea is one which, in principle, is well worth pursuing. He would prefer to avoid superimposing any emblem on the tricolour and to adopt instead some other design distinct from the National Flag …

There followed an exhaustive exchange of views among senior officials about possible designs. As was the pattern in the debate about a state coat of arms, which was just then reaching its conclusion, this debate was confined to civil servants and those whom they chose to consult. There was no public debate of any kind, and indeed the general public would not have known that

the matter was being considered. A questionnaire was sent to foreign governments in search of precedents for the design and usage of the flags of heads of state, and submissions – some of them of extraordinary inaccuracy – were also received from selected Irish and British experts.

Although a number of other themes were discussed, including some strikingly original ideas based on Irish mythology (such as McDunphy's own suggestion of four white swans on blue representing the Children of Lir), it was clear that the harp was the only serious contender. The question of the design boiled down to whether it should be on a field of green or of blue. Dogmatic advocates of heraldic orthodoxy insisted that the harp on a blue field already constituted the coat of arms of Ireland, and that this was therefore the only 'correct' flag for a head of state. This assertion was not legally correct at that time, as these arms were not adopted officially until 2 November 1945, and in any case there was no such obligation on the state to comply with heraldic doctrine. However, the repeatedly asserted legitimacy of the blue field, strengthened by the extrinsic fact that the harp on a green field had in the meantime become a popular flag representing the province of Leinster, won the day.

Arguments based on a 'monarchic' conception of the presidency were put forward explicitly and frequently during the debate about the design of the flag and are reflected in the assertion, still sometimes made, that the presidential standard is a 'banner'* of the arms of Ireland. Apart from the fact that this flag antedates the official adoption of the coat of arms and was chosen

---

*In heraldic terminology, a *banner* is a flag having the same design as the shield of a coat of arms, generally used to indicate the presence of the owner of the arms.

through a completely independent process, this concept is clearly based on a direct comparison with the royal standards displayed by monarchies, which are indeed a derivative of the personal banner of arms, reflecting the feudal belief that the state is the ruler's personal property.

A formal decision was made on 29 December 1944, as recorded in the minutes of the Government:

> The Taoiseach having brought the matter to the attention of the Government, it was decided that there should be a Presidential Standard, consisting of a harp on a blue ground. The question of the regulations regarding the use of the Standard was left for settlement by the Taoiseach.

The details of the design now remained to be settled. A full-size flag was manufactured by the Dun Emer Guild for submission to the Government, and McDunphy described it as follows:

> The blue ground is the nearest practicable approximation to that known as St. Patrick's Blue* ... The harp is a replica of that embodied in the Presidential Seal ... The number of strings, as in the seal, is fifteen. The height of the harp is approximately five-eighths of that of the Standard. The harp which is mounted in the hall of the Árus is placed so that the angle between the strings and the sound board is bisected by a vertical. This arrangement, which was decided on after a good deal of experiment, has been chosen for the Standard ...

---

*The term St Patrick's blue, originally given to the light blue of the ribbon of the Order of St Patrick (1783–1922), was later adopted as a pious alternative name for royal blue (a deep central or purplish blue). Following objections from Edward MacLysaght, the term was later officially dropped in favour of azure, which in heraldic terminology means simply blue, and not any particular shade.

This flag was approved by the Government on 13 February 1945. A number of technical decisions were made at the same time, including the decision that the shade of blue employed be called 'St Patrick's blue' and that the strings of the harp be yellow (in settlement of the question raised by Edward MacLysaght, who had insisted that the strings should be white). It was also decided that no action should be taken against the St Stephen's Green Club, Dublin, which had apparently been flying a flag of the same design. McDunphy later received a visit from the secretary of the National Yacht Club (Dún Laoghaire), whose ensign was also identical to the new flag but who undertook to change it.

The Government had decided that the flag should be introduced without delay, not at the same time as the inauguration of the incoming president, Seán T. O'Kelly, who had been the candidate of Fianna Fáil, to avoid giving the flag any partisan associations. The date chosen was 24 May 1945, a month before the inauguration of the second president on 25 June.

A statement announcing the introduction of the flag was drawn up by McDunphy and issued by the Government:

> *Adopting a practice which obtains in other countries, it has been decided that there shall be a distinctive Presidential Standard, and the official inauguration will take place at Árus an Uachtaráin at 11 to-morrow morning.*
>
> *… The Standard will be reserved to the President and may not be used except with his permission. It will fly over the Árus whenever he is in residence and, when appropriate, over other buildings or at other places whenever he is present. It will always be flown in conjunction with the National Flag, which will be given the place of honour.*

The design is that of the national emblem, the harp, in gold, on a ground of St. Patrick's Blue. The harp is a replica of that on the Presidential Seal, and is represented with fifteen strings. It appears as mirror images on the two sides of the Standard, the curved fore-pillar or lámh-chrann in each case being next to the pole.

The blue ground of the Standard and the gold of the harp are of wool bunting, now manufactured for the first time in Ireland …

On the morning of the twenty-fourth a small party assembled on the lawn of Áras an Uachtaráin, including Dr Hyde, Éamon de Valera and other members of the Government, to watch the hoisting of the presidential standard for the first time.

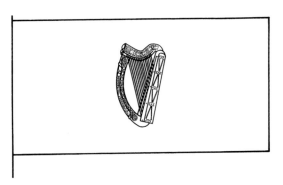

The presidential standard, 1945 to date.

SIX

A COAT OF ARMS

From the early years of the Irish Free State, the government found itself under pressure to adopt a national coat of arms. A state emblem was adopted first, although in a rather haphazard way, and this was (and is) used in all the ways in which such an emblem can be. But not everyone was satisfied with the outcome.

A letter of 19 November 1928 from the secretary of the Department of External Affairs to the secretary of the Executive Council pointed out that

> frequent inquiries on the subject of the coat of arms of the Saorstát are received in this Department. In order that we may be in a position to deal with these enquiries, I am to request you to be good enough to supply me with a few copies of the official national symbol which could be used for reproduction purposes.[1]

Eventually a decision was made on the form of official emblem to be used on stationery and publications. A letter of 26 January 1929 from the Executive Council to the Department of External Affairs records:

> The crest [sic] for official notepaper has now been approved by the Executive Council and will presumably be available to Departments in due course ...

Despite the inaccurate wording of the letter, the device adopted was a line drawing of the harp, with no background or accompanying details – essentially the design of the Percy Metcalfe harp from the coinage introduced in 1928 and similar to the state emblem in use today.

The Department of External Affairs continued to receive a steady stream of overseas enquiries from people who took it for granted that a country within what might be called the heraldic sphere of influence and, more specifically, within the British empire, should adopt a coat of arms that conformed to the conventions of western European and especially of English heraldry. The implicit and sometimes explicit theme of many of these enquiries was that the Free State was under an obligation to adopt a 'proper' coat of arms, and that its failure to do so was an oversight.

There was in fact no such necessity. The only requirements of a state emblem are that it symbolise in an acceptable way the country it represents and that it be used consistently. Indeed a case might be made for rejecting the use of English-style state heraldry, not merely by inertia but deliberately – as many former colonial states have since done – to symbolise the rejection of the values and culture of colonialism. An emblem that was perceived as authentic and as conforming to native norms – which in effect is what was adopted – could have been regarded as a symbol of a state attempting to develop a new, non-colonial culture. The Irish Free State, however, was not such a state, and its politicians and civil servants (with some notable exceptions) would have been slow to suggest that it should be.

Nevertheless, it must be acknowledged that the state emblem as it developed, consisting of a bare black-and-white drawing of the harp, falls short of what most people would expect or like a national emblem to be, particularly in its irregular shape (which was to cause endless problems with orientation) and the absence of colour. The desire to see the adoption of a 'proper' coat of arms no doubt reflected, however incoherently, these aspirations as well.

A letter of 15 May 1931 from the Department of External Affairs to the Executive Council pointed out that

> *the Minister for External Affairs [Patrick McGilligan] is aware that no Coat of Arms has been prescribed for the Irish Free State. The Brian Boru Harp is, however, in use as the official emblem shown without a shield and without any arrangement of colours … Enquiries are constantly being received in this Department as to the design of the Coat of Arms and the colours, and consideration might well be given in due course to having available an authoritative design and colours.*

The acknowledgement to this letter, dated 13 June 1931, repeated the standard formula – 'I have to inform you that the usual reply to enquiries of this nature is to the effect that no Coat of Arms has been adopted for the Irish Free State but that the Brian Boru Harp is the official national symbol.' But on the same date, the secretary of the Executive Council wrote also to Thomas Ulick Sadleir, deputy head of the Office of Arms:[2]

> *We receive from time to time enquiries as to what is the Coat of Arms of the Irish Free State and our usual reply is that no Coat of Arms has yet been adopted but that the Brian Boru Harp is the official national symbol.*

The question will, no doubt, arise for decision some time and for this purpose it would be desirable to have before us a memorandum containing any information which is available …

Assuming that the Harp referred to above might be adopted as the central scheme of a Coat of Arms of this State I would be glad to learn if any information is available which would enable a decision to be made as to the shield or background, both as regards shape and colour which would be appropriate, if at all necessary, or in the absence of any heraldic or historic guidance, whether you have any views on the matter.

It is an interesting comment on the highest officials of the Irish Free State that they would choose to address their enquiries on the national emblem and its history to a member of the English 'royal household' rather than to Irish antiquarians or historians (despite the precedent of the consulting of George Sigerson by Hugh Kennedy in 1922). But in this instance, the state's acknowledged ignorance was matched by that of the supposed authority. Appearing to believe that the official query concerned a design for a flag, which it manifestly did not, Sadleir – after giving a potted history of the harp as used on Anglo-Irish coins and British flags, without replying at all to the query about a coat of arms – asserted:

As regards colour, the Irish flag has always been blue … If a new flag is to be instituted it would seem desirable to retain the blue shield with the golden harp, either in the centre, or at the top flag-staff corner.

In point of fact, no blue 'Irish flag' has ever existed. No action, however, was taken on the basis of this advice or otherwise; and although the question of a coat of arms may have occupied the minds of officials from time to time, it was another fourteen years before any decision was made.

The impetus this time came from Dr Edward MacLysaght, the distinguished scholar and first head of the Genealogical Office. In 1945, he pointed out to Maurice Moynihan, secretary of the Department of the Taoiseach, that no official coat of arms for Ireland was registered in the Office of Arms. (In fact, the first head of that office, Bartholomew Butler, had indeed recorded the blue shield with yellow harp as the arms of Ireland some time in the 1540s, but Butler's papers are in Trinity College Library and not in the Genealogical Office.³) MacLysaght wrote to Moynihan:

> *My authority to act for the Government in heraldic matters is sufficient to enable me to register Arms on my own responsibility but it seems to me that it is a point upon which I should obtain formal approval.*

MacLysaght's unilateral interpretation of his powers was, understandably, viewed with some alarm by the Government. However, he put forward a number of suggestions for their consideration, including the quartered arms of the four provinces as well as the harp. To objections by the Government and some of its advisers that the harp was part of the royal arms of Britain, MacLysaght argued that

> *the kings of England once quartered the Arms of France, a country over which the English have long since ceased to exercise any control. The dignity of the harp as the heraldic emblem of Ireland is not diminished any more than the fleur-de-lis as the emblem of France. In both cases the emblem is older than the British connection [we now*

know that, as far as Ireland is concerned, this is not quite accurate] and lasted after it.

Moynihan eventually submitted a memorandum to the members of the Government on behalf of Éamon de Valera.

The Taoiseach's attention has recently been drawn to the fact that the Arms which are generally used and recognised as those of Ireland are not officially registered in the Genealogical Office ... The Taoiseach recommends that the Government issue a direction to the effect that these Arms be officially registered at the Genealogical Office ...

A formal decision was taken by the Government on 2 November 1945:

Official drawing of the coat of arms, 1947. [National Archives.]

Registration of arms of Ireland: An order was made directing that the Arms Azure a harp or stringed argent* *be officially registered at the Genealogical Office as the Arms of Ireland.*[4]

This coat of arms was duly recorded in the Genealogical Office on 9 November 1945.[5]

It is noteworthy that the processes by which official decisions were arrived at to employ the harp – first on

---

*In plain English: blue, a yellow harp with white strings.

seals, then on coins, then on the presidential standard – took place independently of each other and in no planned sequence and never involved more than an executive decision to use 'a harp' as the 'national emblem'. And these processes all took place before the official adoption of a coat of arms – although of course they were influenced by knowledge of the prior existence of the coat of arms attributed to Ireland.

For some inexplicable reason, it was over a year before a public announcement was made about the adoption of the coat of arms. A press statement drafted by MacLysaght, together with an official drawing prepared under his supervision, was issued by the Government in January 1947 – only to be the subject of another minor controversy, this time about the number and orientation of the strings of the harp.

The debate began with 'An Irishman's Diary' in *The Irish Times* of 3 January 1947, written by Quidnunc (Patrick Campbell). He lampooned the coat of arms under the heading 'The strings are false' and pointed out, among other things, that the harp was oriented in such a way that the strings were not vertical, as they were on Government stationery. This was followed in the same newspaper by an equally silly piece by Myles na gCopaleen (Brian O'Nolan) in his own column.

On official stationery and publications, the harp has nearly always been printed with an orientation in which the strings are vertical. In the absence of any other explanation, it seems probable that this was a crude device used by officials or by printers who, without the guidance of a shield or any other framework, chose the straight lines presented by the strings as the basis for a rule of thumb for placing the emblem on the page. If an aesthetic rather than mechanical criterion is used and the harp is visually balanced, as in traditional drawings, the strings will be at a considerable angle from the vertical.

Among those who decided to take these criticisms seriously was Dr Nicholas Nolan, assistant secretary of the Department of the Taoiseach. MacLysaght (through the secretary of the Department of Education) replied to Nolan's enquiry on 23 January 1947:

> *The normal heraldic practice is to place [the harp] as it appears in the sketch reproduced in the newspapers which results in the strings being in a diagonal direction … To place it at the angle shown on the notepaper referred to would give a decidedly lopsided effect and spoil the symmetry of the coat of arms.*

In his reply, Nolan asserted that if the pattern of harp as used in the coat of arms was

> *by any chance the harp in the British Royal standard, that is one very good reason for not following 'accepted heraldic practice',*

and further that it was

> *absurd that a sovereign State should in effect be told that it is not at liberty to regard a particular harp as its coat of arms because some obscure English knight may have adopted a harp with tilted strings as his coat of arms perhaps seven centuries ago, and thereby set the standard for everyone else.*

Despite MacLysaght's strenuous objections, Nolan's argument carried the day, and a new drawing was prepared in the Genealogical Office showing thirty strings and with an orientation of the harp that caused them to be vertical. This was approved by the Government on 13 June 1947. A colour reproduction of this version was printed in leaflet form and used as the basis for subsequent official drawings; and 'decidedly lopsided' it is.

Revised version of the coat of arms, 1947.

SEVEN

THE HARP
EMBLEM TODAY

The history of the Irish harp emblem is a long and complex one, with many political and ideological aspects. Our knowledge of its earliest years is far from complete.

Despite the formal adoption of the coat of arms in 1945, the plain, uncoloured drawing of a harp continues to be used virtually exclusively as the state emblem. Official documents and publications, public notices, seals, coins, passports, uniform badges – all bear the simple harp device. The adoption of the coat of arms now appears to have been little more than a formality, pressed on the Government by interested parties, and indeed its very existence is unknown to the general public; it would seem that the Fianna Fáil governments of the 1940s were even more susceptible to arguments based on heraldic legitimism than the Cumann na nGaedheal governments of the 1920s.

Some contemporary versions of the state emblem.

It should hardly be necessary to point out that neither the traditional use of the blue coat of arms nor its official adoption in 1945 could – even if it purported to – change the national colour from green to blue. Yet this extraordinary assertion is occasionally made, and one of the official guides to the State Apartments in Dublin Castle can announce that 'contrary to popular belief, the national colour of Ireland is not green but blue.' (It is not clear how a country could have a 'national' colour 'contrary to popular belief'.)

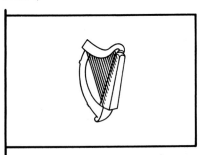

The jack of the Naval Service, 1947 to date, derived from the old national flag.

In 1947, the Green Flag was given a new lease of life in a restricted field when it was adopted as the jack* of the Naval Service.

Another interesting official use of the harp has been its display in a bronze wall-plaque, on an oval shield and with a motto-ribbon bearing the word *Éire*, which for many years has been a feature of such official buildings as court-houses and post offices, as well as of Irish embassies.[1] Although they are still routinely issued to embassies by the Office of Public Works, in recent years these wall-plaques have given way in other areas to the more trendy signs adopted by public corporations, especially

---

*A *jack* is an identifying flag of naval ships, flown at the bow. In some countries it is the same as the national flag; in others a historic national flag or a unique design is used.

those of An Post. It has not been possible to find out whether this plaque was introduced before or after 1945. If before 1945, the placing of the harp on a shield with an accompanying motto-ribbon would seem to suggest that it was intended to be a coat of arms, but with no particular colours (although in recent years some of them have been painted blue); if after 1945, it contradicts the pattern of the coat of arms officially adopted at that time.

In recent years, a number of state organisations have independently adopted official devices based on the harp. The Croatian sculptor Ivan Meštrović was among those invited to submit designs for the coinage in September 1926. Through a mistake, he missed the deadline for the competition but he presented his design for the obverse to the state; it shows a harp held by a human figure. In December 1965, this model was adopted by the Central Bank of Ireland as its seal.

The Government wall-plaque on a post office (Blackrock, Co. Dublin) in 1990. [Éilis McDonnell]

The National Gallery of Ireland uses a motif from Francis Fowke's design for the frieze in the Sculpture Hall of the gallery, dating from 1861, consisting of a decorative harp within a wreath.[2] The use by statutory bodies of a harp device differentiated in various ways from that of the state emblem introduces an elegant diversity to a familiar motif and demonstrates that the centuries-old harp emblem is still capable of creative adaptation.

Seal of the Central Bank, 1965 to date, based on the coin designs of Ivan Meštrović.

Emblem of the National Gallery of Ireland.

REFERENCES

1. THE IRISH HARP

1. Extracts from official records relating to the design of state seals are reproduced from the National Archives, file S1587, by permission of the deputy keeper.

2. The principal technical accounts of the harp include *Musical Instruments, Part 1: The Irish and the Highland Harps* by Robert Bruce Armstrong (David Douglas, Edinburgh, 1904; facsimile reprint as *The Irish and Highland Harps*, Irish University Press, Shannon, 1969) and *The Irish Harp* (third edition) by Joan Rimmer (Mercier Press, Cork, 1984).

3. Dáithí Ó hÓgáin, *Myth, Legend and Romance: An Encyclopaedia of the Irish Folk Tradition* (Ryan Publishing, London, 1990).

4. John Derricke, *The Image of Ireland with a Discoverie of Wood Kearne* (London, 1581).

5. Raphael Holinshed, *The Chronicles of England, Scotlande, and Irelande to the Yeare 1586 ...* (second edition, London, 1587), chap. 8. The Irish chapter was in fact compiled by Edmond Campion in 1570–71 and rewritten by Richard Stanihurst.

6. Seán O'Boyle, *The Irish Song Tradition* (Gilbert Dalton, Dublin, 1976), p. 10.

7. From a manuscript history of Ireland, *c.* 1610, in the Royal Irish Academy, Dublin (ms. 24 G.15, p. 21), quoted by James Hardiman in

Irish Minstrelsy, or Bardic Remains of Ireland, with English Translations, vol. 1 (Joseph Robins, London, 1831; facsimile reprint, Irish University Press, Shannon, 1971), p. 183.

8. 'The present state of Ireland', *Journal of the Royal Society of Antiquaries of Ireland*, vol. 5 (1875), p. 179.

2.   A SYMBOL OF IRELAND

1. Breac Mhaodhóg is in the National Museum, Dublin. The bronze figures, about 2 inches (50 mm) high, are believed to have been made between 1050 and 1100.

2. The Wijnbergen Armorial is in the custody of the Koninklijk Genootschap voor Geslacht en Wapenkunde (Royal Genealogy and Heraldry Society), Den Haag, but its owners do not allow it to be examined or photographed, and all attempts to obtain a photograph of the relevant portion were frustrated. It has been reproduced, however, in *Un Armorial Français du XIIIe Siècle: L'Armorial Wijnbergen* by Paul Adam-Even and Léon Jéquier (offprint from *Archives Héraldiques Suisses*, Neuchâtel, 1954), which includes a photograph of folio 35r, containing the coat of arms attributed to Ireland. Our illustration is based on a photocopy of this offprint kindly supplied by M. Jéquier and on a copy provided by Dr John Kennedy, Toronto.

3. Quoted by Rimmer, *The Irish Harp*, p. 41.

4. J. Bernard Burke, *Vicissitudes of Families*, vol. 1 (Burke's Peerage, London, 1869), p. 125.

5. College of Arms ms. 12.

6. Seaby 4472–4478. (Coin references are to the standard catalogue, *Coins and Tokens of Ireland* by Peter Seaby (Seaby, London, 1970).)

7.   Michael Dolley, 'The harp on Anglo-Irish coins: a preliminary exposition', *Numismatic Society of Ireland: Occasional Papers*, no. 10–14 (Jan. 1970), p. 1–10. I am indebted to Derek Young for this reference.

8.   In *An Itinerary … thorow Twelve Dominions* (London, 1617).

9.   The shield bearing three crowns does indeed appear on an Anglo-Irish silver farthing of *c.* 1467–70 (Seaby 4404) and later coins, *c.* 1483–90 (Seaby 4412–4446), though arranged vertically, and not on a shield.

10.   The Ryther map is in the National Maritime Museum, London; it is reproduced on the jacket of *The Weidenfeld Atlas of Maritime History* by Richard Natkiel and Antony Preston (Weidenfeld and Nicolson, London, 1986).

11.   The various ornamental versions of the harp are surveyed by G.A. Hayes-McCoy in *A History of Irish Flags from Earliest Times* (Academy Press, Dublin, 1979), p. 46–47.

3. THE GREEN FLAG

1.   The O'Hartegan letter is in the Franciscan Institute of Celtic Studies and Historical Research (Killiney, County Dublin), vol. D4, p. 849, and is reprinted in the Historical Manuscripts Commission's *Report on Franciscan Manuscripts …* (Historical Manuscripts Commission, Dublin, 1906), p. 208.

2.   The flag of the Waterford Regiment of the Spanish army *c.* 1701–13 was plain green with a yellow harp; see Terence Wise, *Military Flags of the World* (Blandford Press, Poole, 1977), plate 21.

3.   The early references to green as a colour symbolising Ireland are surveyed by Brian Ó Cuív in 'The wearing of the green', *Studia Hibernica*, no. 17–18 (1977–78), p. 107–119. Prof. Ó Cuív comments: 'I am ready to concede that for many centuries blue has had particular

significance in relation to Ireland in the context of heraldry. However, I suggest that there we are dealing with the Ireland of English kings and their adherents.'

4. Risteard Ó Foghludha (editor), *Cois na Bríde: Liam Inglis OSA, 1709–88: A Chuid Filíochta* (Stationery Office, Dublin, 1937), p. 27.

5. Seaby 4555–4559.

6. Seaby 4567, 4568.

7. The history of the shamrock emblem is recounted in detail by E. Charles Nelson in *Shamrock: Botany and History of an Irish Myth* (Boethius Press, Kilkenny, 1991).

8. 'On Monday, St. Patrick's day, at Witham, in Essex, where are billeted some of the Irish soldiers, they after their country manner wearing in their hats red riband crosses ...' From a letter of 21 March 1628 from an unknown correspondent to Rev. Joseph Mead, secretary to Archbishop Laud, quoted in *The Court and Times of Charles the First* (Henry Colburn, London, 1848), vol. 1, p. 331.

9. The identification of this device with Uí Briain of Thomond has been put forward convincingly by Dr John Kennedy of Toronto.

10. The notebook of William Downman is in the National Maritime Museum, London (ms. NVT/8); the relevant pages are also reproduced in *Flags at Sea* by Timothy Wilson (HMSO, London, 1986), p. 68, which also reproduces other early manuscript illustrations of the same flag.

11. Flags of the Volunteers are extensively described and illustrated by Hayes-McCoy in *A History of Irish Flags*, p. 83–99.

12. Stella Tillyard, *Citizen Lord: Edward Fitzgerald, 1763–1798* (Chatto and Windus, London, 1997), p. 158, 179–80.

13. National Archives, Rebellion Papers, 620/37/99, quoted by Thomas Pakenham in *The Year of Liberty: The Story of the Great Irish Rebellion of 1798* (Hodder and Stoughton, London, 1969), p. 85.

14. Tillyard, *Citizen Lord*, p. 258.

15. The flags of the 1798 revolutionaries are analysed in detail by Hayes-McCoy, *A History of Irish Flags*, p. 114–18.

16. A detailed though biased description of the 1798 leaders in County Wexford is given by Charles Jackson in *A Narrative of the Sufferings and Escape of Charles Jackson* ... (London, 1798), p. 19, and by other contemporary accounts.

17. The extract from Tone's diary is reproduced in *The Autobiography of Theobald Wolfe Tone, 1763–1798*, edited by R. Barry O'Brien (Unwin, London, 1893), vol. 2, p. 52.

18. The letter of the Directory to Hoche is in the Archives de la Guerre, Paris, file B5*-97, folio 78v (letter 218), translated by F. van Brock in 'A proposed Irish regiment and standard, 1796', *Irish Sword*, vol. 11 (1973–74), p. 231.

19. Marianne Elliott, *Wolfe Tone: Prophet of Irish Independence* (Yale University Press, New Haven, 1989), p. 362.

20. Elliott, *Wolfe Tone*, p. 389.

21. Reproduced by Thomas Pakenham in *The Year of Liberty*, facing p. 128.

22. Our illustration of Emmet's flag is based on a contemporary drawing reproduced by H.F.B. Wheeler and A.M. Broadley in *The War in Wexford ... in 1798: Told from Original Documents* (Bodley Head, London, 1910), facing p. 294.

23. Emmet's draft manifesto is printed in *History of the Irish Rebellion in 1798* by W.H. Maxwell (A.H. Baily and Company, London, 1845), p. 472.

24. Hayes-McCoy, *A History of Irish Flags*, p. 23.

25. In *A History of Irish Flags*, plate 1 (facing p. 33), Prof. Hayes-McCoy shows a colour photograph of what is clearly a commercially manufactured flag of the harp-and-canton type with a post-1801 Union Jack canton and records that he saw such a flag flying in London in 1934.

26. Hayes-McCoy, *A History of Irish Flags*, plate 1 (facing p. 33), illustrates a version of the Lord Lieutenant's flag with a crown over the shield. This also is a photograph of a real flag, although none of the nineteenth-century flag charts nor Admiralty flag books show such a version.

27. *The Irish Volunteer*, vol. 1, no. 16 (23 May 1914), p. 15.

28. *The Irish Volunteer* (new series), vol. 2, no. 15 (20 Mar. 1915), p. 4.

29. *The Workers' Republic*, no. 48 (22 Apr. 1916).

30. C. Desmond Greaves, *The Life and Times of James Connolly* (Lawrence and Wishart, London, 1961), p. 403; Samuel Levenson, *James Connolly: A Biography* (Martin Brian and O'Keeffe, London, 1973), p. 292.

31. The evidence for the flags displayed during 1916 is examined in detail by Hayes-McCoy in *A History of Irish Flags*, p. 209–215.

4.   STATE SEALS

1. The Four Provinces stamp was designed by Millicent Girling, a teacher at the Metropolitan School of Art (now the National College of Art and Design), Dublin. A public competition was organised on 1 February 1922 for the first postage stamps of the Irish Free State, and four designs were chosen from the 129 entries. The Four Provinces stamp was introduced in three denominations in September and October 1923 and remained in use until 1937, and was issued again

between 1940 and 1968. The stamp on p. 36 is reproduced by kind permission of An Post © 1998.

2. In a letter to the author, the late Mr Scott-Giles said that the reason he gave the Four Provinces shield as the arms of Ireland was its use on postage stamps.

3. National Archives, file S1587.

4. The process of creating the seal of the Irish Free State is described by Hugh Kennedy in an article, 'The Great Seal of Saorstát Éireann', published in the Christmas 1924 issue of the *Irish Sketch and Lady of the House.*

5. The Trinity College harp is on permanent display in the Long Room of the Old Library, Trinity College, Dublin; a replica is in the Music Room of the National Museum. The photograph on p. 38 is reproduced by permission of the Board of Trinity College, Dublin. A detailed description of the harp is given in the exhibition catalogue *Treasures of Early Irish Art, 1500 BC to 1500 AD* (Metropolitan Museum of Art, New York, 1977), p. 218–19, as well as in *The Irish Harp* by Joan Rimmer.

6. Yeats's proposals and the quotations from correspondence between Yeats and Hugh Kennedy and between Kennedy and Alice Stopford Green were published in 'Had I the heavens' embroidered cloths: Yeats's role in robing the judiciary' by Ronan Keane in *The Irish Times,* 'Weekend' supplement, 9 June 1990, p. 2–3, which includes reproductions of some of the original drawings, all from the Archives Department, University College, Dublin. The extract from the Yeats letter is reproduced by kind permission of Micheál Yeats.

7. The extracts from the proceedings of the coinage committee are from 'Summary of the proceedings of the Committee' by Leo

McCauley (secretary of the committee) in *Coinage of Saorstát Éireann, 1928* (Stationery Office, Dublin, 1928), p. 19–53.

8. The illustration of the presidential seal is reproduced from *The President of Ireland: His Powers, Functions and Duties* by Michael McDunphy (Browne and Nolan, Dublin, 1945), facing p. 98. Extracts from official records relating to the presidential seal are reproduced from the National Archives, file S10200A, by permission of the deputy keeper.

5. THE PRESIDENTIAL STANDARD

1. Extracts from official records relating to the adoption of the presidential standard are reproduced from the National Archives, file S13513A, by permission of the deputy keeper.

6. A COAT OF ARMS

1. Extracts from official records relating to the adoption of a coat of arms are reproduced from the National Archives, file S5383A, by permission of the deputy keeper.

2. The Office of Arms in Dublin Castle was technically part of the English 'royal household' rather than a department of the British government, and for this reason it was not abolished on the establishment of the Irish Free State in 1922. This anomalous position was allowed to continue until 1 April 1943, when (following the death of the incumbent) the institution was transformed into the Genealogical Office and placed under the jurisdiction of the Department of Education, in practice as a subdivision of the National Library. These decisions were made by the Government on its own initiative (Government Order no. 267 of 1943) and later given

statutory recognition by Section 13 of the National Cultural Institutions Act (1997).

3.   I am indebted to Dr John Kennedy, Toronto, for this information.

4.   Government minutes, National Archives, file G.4/100, item 1, reproduced by permission of the deputy keeper.

5.   Genealogical Office, Register of Arms, vol. Q, folio 20.

7.   THE HARP EMBLEM TODAY

1.   Additional information on the Government wall-plaque was kindly supplied by Chris Flynn, information officer of the Office of Public Works.

2.   The National Gallery emblem is reproduced by courtesy of the National Gallery of Ireland.

ALSO AVAILABLE FROM WOLFHOUND PRESS

The Wolfhound Guide to
Dublin Monuments

Elizabeth Healy

Packed with information on dozens of monuments, many of which have become so familiar to Dubliners that we have stopped noticing them. This book looks at how the monuments, memorials, statues, public sculptures and corporate art of Dublin reflect the history of the city and that of the nation.

ISBN 0 86327 637 7

The Wolfhound Guide to
The River Gods

Elizabeth Healy

Atlantic, Bann, Barrow, Blackwater, Boyne, Erne, Foyle, Lagan, Lee, Liffey, Nore, Slaney, Shannon, Suir – these are the River Gods, the riverine heads decorating the arches of Dublin's Custom House. This book chronicles their creation by sculptor Edward Smyth and provides a short history of each of the rivers, with a description of their geography and place in Irish culture.

ISBN 0 86327 642 3

The Wolfhound Guide to
The Irish Wolfhound

Muriel Monsell Bremner

A treasure trove of everything you ever wanted to know about this great dog's close identity with Ireland's history, plus lots of interesting things you never thought to ask. Renowned for their strength, famed for their courage and cherished for their sensitivity and loyalty, these dogs have been immortalised in legend and song.

ISBN 0 86327 636 9
